Monkeys in the Jungle:

A Parable of Trees that Just Won't Grow

Jesse Steele

Amazon Paperback Edition

Copyright © 2015 Jesse Steele

All rights reserved. No part of this book may be reproduced for sale in any manner whatsoever without written permission of the author except in the case of brief quotations embodied in critical articles and reviews.

books.jessesteele.com
books@jessesteele.com

ISBN 978-1798534656

For my Hometown

Table of Contents

Introduction A:
The Steele Theorem of Decline   iii

Introduction B:
Why Some Trees Just Won't Grow   ix

Roots First   1

The Parable   4

Present-Day Application   12

Conclusion   24

About the Author   28

Introduction A: The Steele Theorem of Decline

The parable in this book does not directly connect to the five phases of the Steele Theorem of Decline. But, by understanding the basic phases of the Theorem, the reader will see the Theorem at work in the parable.

The cyclical phases of the Steele Theorem of Decline:

Phase 1. Organic Health: Good, ordinary people develop good things, unofficially, and without central planning. They focus on intrinsic quality and are somewhat rough around the edges, but their products and ideas are sticky, catchy, and they last. In marketing, they gain momentum and longevity. These are original visionaries. Their "organization" can be a fellowship, business, charity, school, or even a nation.

Phase 2. Certified Validation: Once good things are established, it is suggested by someone that it is desirable to institutionalize and centralize organizational structures for better "efficiency". "Accreditation" and "certification" are also discussed as a means of ensuring that the masses are not deceived by copycats. This new discussion often accompanies an inward desire for "validation" and "to be important" and "to be recognized" for the good things one has done. This inward desire is often not acknowledged by the people who have it. Rather, the hidden attitude manifests itself with pious, calm, friendly comments such as, "It really is good, ya know. Doors will open this way. Everything needs to institutionalize. It's a necessary evil." While some structures may be valuable and necessary for any organization to progress, as requirements they are minimal and many times they are mere "artificial needs" created during an unnecessary increase of regulation.

Phase 3. *Momentum and Latter Management:* The institutionalized structures attract new leaders* with no vision relating to the original founding. Some or one of these latter managers usually emerges in Phase Two, unnoticed and usually praising the unofficial work of the original visionaries done in Phase One. Many times, they convince themselves that they support the original goals of the founding because they misunderstand what those original goals were. These latter managers focus on aesthetics and smooth operations. Some qualities improve slightly; many things get polished. Growth continues, but it is difficult for many to distinguish whether the continued growth was caused by the early visionaries or the latter managers. During this phase, skeletons pile up in the closets that few people discover until near the end of Phase Four. Some key leaders may resign with no other indications that there is any problem. Those who complain are easily branded as "rebels", "alarmists", "doomsayers", and "malcontents" who "just want attention" and who "really have nothing to complain about".

Phase 4. Abandon Ship: The original visionaries leave, due to a variety of reasons and usually by scattering with the occasional organized exodus. The new, latter managers take over and manage the organization's decline**. They focus on whatever their talking points may be as whatever they manage continues to decline. In the transition to this phase, the original "drive" grows absent and the former momentum eventually turns to a downhill roll that ends in a train wreck. The numbers are typically reported by the organization as being "good". Accountants and researchers may begin to falsify reports or consider falsifying reports during this phase. Original founding members from phase one may begin to share stories through their informal grapevine as they unofficially network. The organization's bad reputation emerges slowly and finally culminates in a public announcement of some legal action or negative report in the press, but the problems of the organization rarely surprise those who have a close connection to the organization's history. The latter managers usually erect power structures in this phase, such as retirement packages, mergers and acquisitions, and outside contracts. These obligations are designed to remain in place even after the organization is no longer solvent since insolvency was foreseen by the latter managers. Intentional or otherwise, these "safety nets" serve in helping the latter managers survive as the organization flounders through either bankruptcy, liquidation, or acquisition. Near the end of phase four, the phase-three "rebels" are turned to for advice and many of their disloyal friends seek reconciliation with them.

Phase 5. *Reassembly:* The visionaries informally congregate and discuss philosophies about their situation and general life lessons learned. They share wisdom from their own lives and from the annals of history. They create a new, unofficial organization with devices in place to avoid the style and manner of the most recent takeover of the latter managers. They wrest much of the remaining power from the latter managers, but not all. Then the cycle repeats with their new, good work. In some cases, the original visionaries return to the organization and retake control, which resets the organization to "Phase One Prime" where the same cycle may repeat at a more dramatic level with the same, "retaken" organization.

Often, the "latter managers" operate in some form of cooperation with hostile forces or undisclosed or unacknowledged motives. Many times, this involves ordinary folk who desire the greatness described in Phase Two. Other times, Phase Two is implemented by an insurgent who pretends to be a founder, but secretly harbors associates hostile to the organization. These "conscious cooperators" usually act under the direction of a respected and known "secret society" such as in collage fraternities, business clubs, or any of the many respected secret societies known throughout Europe. Conscious cooperators are not always involved, however, and typically focus on influencing larger and more famous organizations.

**There is usually general disgust with the latter managers, arising in Phase Four. However, there is rarely any acknowledgement that the problem originated with "subtle pride" desire for greatness and validation that emerged in Phase Two. Most people, whether the latter managers or the visionaries, including their respective supporters, are able to identify when the problems first began. They usually point to events in Phase Three when fixing retrospective blame.*

It should be noted that the power to create within the organization lies only with the original visionaries of Phase One. The latter managers are demonstrably incapable of beginning a new work with their talking points and ideals, but only polish a pre-created work while the old momentum lasts. The latter managers, in this way, are somewhat of the "hermit crabs" of society. The original visionaries, however, are very strong and capable because they have creative power that latter managers lack. Though they often prefer informal means, are unrefined and somewhat quirky and loony, they have living proof that they should remain confident in their work. Often times, insulting one's "lack of manners" is a dubious attempt to make the original visionaries feel inferior when they have every reason not to. Of course, none of this changes the fact that weaknesses and shortcomings of the original visionaries do cause pragmatic obstacles, which prove room for needed learning. In the case of a fifth phase of "Reassembly", the original visionaries usually return having learned valuable lessons, more mature, and having overcome their shortcomings.

Introduction B:
Why Some Trees Just Won't Grow

Why do problems seem immortal? How come no answer ever seems to be good enough? Why do people fight when, in principle, they actually agree? And why do these sorts of problems plague every sect of society, from business to government to religion?

This book tells a parable that seeks to answer these questions. It is based on the Steele Theorem of Decline, explained in the Introduction. The Theorem can't be proven, but it works and can accurately predict unfolding history. The parable begins with a background of Fallen Angels and bamboo trees.

There are many Fallen Angels. Some are known; some are not. One of them operates with the alias Lucifer, but there is no Biblical evidence to suggest that this is or ever was his actual name nor that Angels know him by this name. The serpent in the Garden of Eden was likely not the most powerful of the Fallen Angels, but is the dragon and cause of much evil in the Book of Revelation. Other Fallen Angels appear in Revelation, such as Appolyon. But answering the question of which Fallen Angel is the main source of earthly mischief is neither important to the parable nor the Theorem. In fact, it shouldn't really be important to anyone.

The important thing—and, really, the only reason making it worth mention at all—is that, being based in witchcraft, the evilest of men need not be feared because Jesus is more powerful than the Fallen Angels who give them their power. But, to access Jesus's power, one must watch and pray for wisdom and strength to face the problems of the day.

The prime, deep, rood factor of earthly mischief is that there is always a plurality of collaborative efforts of Fallen Angelic princes, remotely involved in almost every human conflict. Usually, those Fallen Angels work with more than one group of humans, telling each that they are the group they favor. Actually, the Fallen Angels are just watching to see whichever human group conquers the others. That collective satanic-accusing force of Fallen Angels is aliased by this parable as the Tigers, where Tigers has a capital "T". The problems presented as questions in the first paragraph are referred to as "mischief" in the jungle.

In reality, the Tigers represent a group of evil spiritual beings that are known in the Bible as "Satans" which means "Accusers" because "accusing" was how they began their rebellion and they never stopped. These are also known as the fallen "Watchers" of Noah's time. In real life, the Watchers always maintain a direct relationship with a few, various small groups of humans who are the center of mischief on the earth, just how the Tigers maintain a connection to some, not all, of the Monkeys. In the parable, the Tigers are the menace behind the Monkeys in the jungle, but can only create the mischief as long as the Monkeys cooperate. In the real world and when those humans die, then the Fallen Angels will seek out other unwitting humans to serve as their new toadies. So, knowing which specific group of Monkeys happens to serve the Tigers at any given time is as irrelevant as knowing which Fallen Angels wicked and selfish men happen to be cooperating with on any given day. The dirty little secret is that all men cooperate with the Fallen Angels, the Watchers, when they sin, though some more than others.

Technically, and it is a conclusion of this parable, any human who participates in evil serves the evil, Fallen Angels, at least in part, wittingly or unwittingly. Just the same, all who serve the Watchers can repent and walk away, but only in the power of Christ Jesus. If a servant of the Watchers tries to break ties with those demonic forces by any power other than Jesus's, they are technically able to be killed through witchcraft. So, there really is only one way out for everyone.

Many conspiracy theorists center their theories about one-world government plots around a specific group of organizations or families. However, another point of this parable is that identifying those humans is irrelevant. The important factor to identify is the behavior, the pattern, and the results. Jesus said, "Ye shall know them by their fruit." It is the identity of fruit that we must be concerned with, not the identities of humans and Angels.

In the parable, the group of humans that collaborate with the Fallen Angels (Watchers, in the parable 'Tigers') to create mischief are called "Monkeys" with a capital "M". In the parable, the Monkeys eat fruit and swing from trees. The Lord God is the Master Farmer.

With those terms set, here is a brief overview of tree farming...

Roots First

Most trees grow in the forest as either hardwoods or softwoods. They grow slowly and steadily, year by year. One can easily guess the age of one of these trees by looking at its thickness and height. Hardwood trees have their own culture. Oak trees drop acorns that make the soil acidic, discouraging other hardwood trees from competing in the same forest. Some pine cones are only unlocked by fire, which is why softwoods are often the beginning of a new forest. But, there is another kind of tree that grows in the forest: bamboo.

Bamboo grows underground first, then above ground. The first stage of growth can take years, depending on the species of bamboo. After developing an extensive root system, in longer cases five years, the bamboo shoot will finally begin to grow. Some grow at a rate of 16 inches per day or even two feet. Some have said that a bamboo shoot can grow so fast that one can "hear" it growing. This shoot growth phase can last about six weeks until the bamboo tree reaches its final height, in some cases 90 feet tall. Then the shoot stops growing tall and the roots continue to expand as the foundation for future shoots.

People are all like tree farmers. Different trees have different inherent skills, given by God, while each farmer makes choices. The Lord will offer people a choice of which tree to grow: a bamboo or hardwood or softwood tree. Softwood trees can only grow after a forest fire. Hardwood trees have continuous, visible growth, but grow slowly. But, for the most part, bamboo trees grow taller than hardwoods and do so within five years, though their growth is not visible until their growth cycle is almost complete.

Depending on one's choices, a person can grow different trees for different purposes. Bamboo farmers may often be despised by others as "not growing" during the early phases where the roots grow and little happens above ground. Similarly, winter is a "leafless" growth phase where hardwoods grow deep to find water. This makes their foundation strong so that, once the leaves bud, the summer winds will not blow the trees down. Every tree is different, but every tree has its value and purpose and roots are the constant hidden growth, the necessity below the surface. The danger for any tree farmer is putting one's tree in a pot.

If a tree is potted, its roots will not be able to expand and, consequentially, neither will the branches above ground. For all trees, branches above ground require roots of near-equal size. Visible growth above ground depends on unseen root growth below ground. The freedom for the roots to grow is a causal factor in a tree's size, while the branches and leaves are the effect of the size of the root system. When a tree is confined to a pot, and the root system is constrained, the tree is will bonsai and stop growing.

The Parable

A farmer grows a tree in the jungle. Because the farmer makes wise choices, the tree grows healthy, strong, and beautiful. But the farmer is young and this is his first tree. He does not know all the secrets of forestry. Because he follows some basic principles of farming taught by the Master Farmer, his tree is fruitful and he prospers. And because he is in his youth, he has received little recognition for his wise choices that he made in secret. His prosperity has also remained mostly a secret.

This farmer could be any age, but his trees are somewhat young. He worked every day, even when no one was watching. If he was growing bamboo, he was probably despised by his neighbors because bamboo does not yield results on the same seasonal schedule of most others. If he grew a hardwood tree, it would have been shorter than older trees, so he would always feel inferior, but would have had the approval of his neighbors. The farmer knew he made wise choices, and, being young, he knew that he had worked more than he was recognized for. In the end, it would have been best if he only concerned himself with the opinion of the Master Farmer, but few ever do.

Soon, the Monkeys approach the tree farmer, often claiming to be a group of philanthropists with good intentions. They begin by praising the farmer for his young trees, giving him great recognition, typically more recognition than he deserves. But, not having due recognition before that point, he accepts their accolades. The fact remains that the Master Farmer instructs everyone to avoid flattery,

Only in rare cases does a farmer follow all the instructions of the Master Farmer, including His instructions to spend large amounts of time in His counsel. The farmers who do this know the Master Farmer's opinion. If the farmer not only worked in the fields, but also prayed, then he would not be susceptible to the Monkey's flattery. But, most farmers only follow the Master Farmer's instructions just enough to make trees grow, not enough to make their hearts grow as well.

So, the farmer of young trees welcomes the friendly comments of the Monkeys. Then, the Monkeys offer to give his trees a "boost". With this "boost", the tree will be higher, will receive extra food and water, and have more sunlight. Because the Monkeys have so many resources, they can make his tree stand out in the forest, even by the end of that same day. But, the farmer must promise to do some work for them, should they ever ask him to, but the Monkeys say that it isn't much work. It mainly consists of allowing them to eat his fruit and swing from the branches of his tree. So it shouldn't be a problem, they claim.

The farmer agrees and the Monkeys put his tree in a pot. Maybe the pot is large. Perhaps it is small. The pot fits the size of the tree so that the tree can live, but it can't grow anymore. The young farmer does not know the danger of potting trees and his newly potted tree is placed on a tall pillar and stands above the forest. The tree does not tower in the forest for the same reason as a tall tree would, but because it has merely been potted and hoisted.

By potting the tree, the Monkeys have placed an invisible ceiling above the tree. If the farmer does not know better, he will always look up to the sky, wondering why his tree no longer grows, but he will only see the sky, not the constrained roots.

As time goes on, and the farmer asks why his tree has not grown. The Monkeys ask him to do more and more work. If he complies, they promise to put the tree in a higher place, but only if he will do more work and not ask questions. As their relationship continues, the Monkeys may even re-pot the tree, making more room for the roots to grow, allowing the tree to gain some size. But, the farmer is no longer doing the work of growing trees. He serves the Monkeys in order for his tree to grow. He is no longer concerned with fruit since the Monkeys eat all his fruit. He is only concerned with the size of his tree, which he no longer waters or cultivates. His work as a farmer is lost and any progress has been bestowed upon him rather than being earned by his own wise choices. By this point, his work has lost its soul because he sold his soul to the Monkeys.

There are other farmers in the Monkeys' potted forest. The Monkeys draw visitors and take farmers hostage with their so-called "prosperity". They lure outsiders by presenting stolen fruit as evidence of their supposed "wisdom". They keep the farmers at odds with each other, making the forest a game of competition. Farmers who please the Monkeys are rewarded with relocated and re-potted trees. And they use their stolen resources to create problems all through the jungle, even for farmers who have never encountered the Monkeys.

This constant system of "competition" keeps the farmers from uniting against the Monkeys. This two-armed tactic of the Tigers allows them to control the Monkeys: create two-sided competition among the Monkeys, with a third group of fringe "loonies". Farmers who don't join the Monkeys in their two-sided competition are considered "outcast" or "strange" and simply left to feel friendless. Two is the magic number of their fake competition and three is the curse.

As time goes on, the Monkeys place more and more burden on the farmer's tree. Eventually, it is too much for the potted tree to handle. Perhaps it can't produce enough fruit. Perhaps it can't support the excessive swinging from the monkeys. Finally, the farmer becomes angry and wants his tree to return to his field. But the Monkeys refuse. If the farmer fights them or if he stops communicating with the Monkeys, the Monkeys kill him and keep his tree for themselves. Many times, even if the farmer does not have a conflict with the Monkeys, they will kill him anyway.

Eventually, the Monkeys destroy a tree and begin to look for another tree to replace it. They don't know how to farm. They don't know how to plant trees. The Monkeys only know how to seduce farmers, pot trees, steal fruit, and jump from limb to limb.

Among their tactics, the Monkeys create two-sided quarrels by inserting different problems among different groups of farmers. This causes farmers to continuously switch between factions, never satisfied with any "solution". The Monkeys speak great truth, while inserting small selections of their propaganda, scattering different ideas among different groups of farmers, but permeating the entire potted forest. Every so often, the Monkeys present a solution to all of the problems they secretly created: that the farmers should trust some of the younger Monkeys "because the handsome, young Monkey will be different from the others". And so the cycle continues.

The farmers rarely consider that the only way to save the jungle is to quickly identify and reject the Monkeys' propaganda, even when it is embedded with great truth and to see that the Monkeys are not the solution to the problems that they secretly created in the first place.

Of course, normally, farmers would not be suspicious of each other. But, this is where the mischief of the Monkeys works its greatest evil. By convincing each farmer that the "other farmer" only wants to hypnotize and deceive him, the Monkeys keep the farmers from communicating. Communication between farmers is what the Monkeys fear most, as that would lead them to discover the truth. But, because the farmers allow themselves to be divided, and tolerate reasons to prevent direct fellowship, the jungle must eventually be destroyed.

But, the Monkeys, blinded by their shortsighted greed, do not see their own method used against them. They themselves are controlled. The Tigers keep two groups of Monkeys fighting against each other, competing with their potted forests. A third group of Monkeys is kept as a fringe group, ready to rise up when, inevitably, one of the two larger

Monkey groups conquers the other. Eventually, when no longer useful to the Tigers, one group of Monkeys is allowed to be eaten by the other group, then the third group of young Monkeys is flattered by the Tigers, told to crush the remaining Monkey group, and that new group inherits the potted forest.

Whether the story of the farmers or the story of the Monkeys, the cycle continues. The Tigers are like parasites that use the Monkeys as a "parasite proxy" through which farmers can be harnessed and enslaved by violating their virtues. The Tigers view the entire jungle as their crop and the inhabitants as their cattle. Collectively, the farmers are stronger than the Monkeys and the Tigers. Were it not for the Monkeys, the Tigers would be seen as they are and the farmers would tame the jungle. But, by not following the wisdom of the Master Farmer fully, the farmers pot their trees, quarrel with each other, and thus the Tigers and their Monkeys create mischief in the jungle, seemingly to no end.

Neither the Monkeys nor the Tigers can touch the Master because is made of fire and has the power of fire. While the jungle can grow back, all inhabitants of the jungle will perish by fire. The only way to end the cycle of the Monkeys in the jungle is for the Master to call out the farmers, along with what

Monkeys will stop serving the Tigers, and burn the entire jungle to the ground.

Neither the Monkeys nor the Tigers nor the farmers can wield such a great fire without being scorched themselves. Only the Master can bring salvation by fire. Until He comes, the farmers do well not to be seduced by the Monkeys. In the end, the Master will hold the farmers responsible—not for being duped by the Monkeys nor for being ignorant about the Tigers, but for taking the shortcut to good results, for trying to cheat time and work.

And, so, the Master will hold the farmers responsible for needing to burn down the jungle, and the mischief of neither the Monkeys nor the Tigers will absolve them because farmers know how to judge according to fruit.

This is a parable about farmers who burned down their jungle.

Present-Day Application

This story explains problems in economics, business, government, and religion. It explains why Atheists fight with Christians and why Christians fight with each other. It explains why Americans quarrel over political issues where one party always wins, but the people always lose. And, it explains why conspiracy theorists waste their time, because God knows the work of the devil, yet expects every individual to judge by the fruit on the tree.

The pots include any institutionalized system. For Christianity, the pot is the weekly system of meetings and clerical definition (rather than Biblical) definition of a pastor. For politics, it is any two-party system. In economics, it is "Capitalism v Hippies".

Many people see Satan's hand at work in one system, but not in the other. Children may grow up believing in free market Capitalism, but then become irritated with "corptocracy" and decide that becoming a Hippie is the solution. But they never see the two-armed approach at work. Those who see the two-armed problem of Capitalism v Hippieism may lunge toward the nearest "third" option. But, as wonderful as that third option seems, and for some "unknown" reason, that third option never succeeds.

"Churchianity" (Christian denominationalism) is another example of the Monkeys, the pots, and the two-handed strategy. Churchianity is full of bureaucracy and abuse. The *95 Theses of the Clerical System* and *Clergy Don't Shepherd* explain this problem in greater depth. In terms of this parable, some people "see the glass as half full" and remain in denominational, clerical Churchianity. Others become irritated and turn away from Jesus altogether. A recently promoted Monkey group is "non-denominationalism", which pretends to be a step in the right direction, while retaining the same bureaucratic system of weekly Churchianity that upholds dogmatic loyalty to systems, traditions, and offices that the Bible never so much as mentions. The "third options" include joining cults, "fads" in Christianity, or become an Atheist. No one ever seems to consider Jesus without the weekly bureaucracy as a viable option.

Other applications of the Monkey parable can be seen in competing news networks. Stories in books and videos often have one good team and one bad team, maybe with a third group. Many comic series give classic examples of the heroes and villains competing. All the while, humanity, for the most part, is left to watch the conflict between comic super heroes and is at most minimally involved, at most.

Internationally, wars are depicted in news as being one side against the other. In WWII, Russia was a US ally. Afterward, that changed, yet no one seemed to ask why—not in the news media anyway. Once this book is published, however, someone in the media will ask, but with no meaningful change to the way wars are covered in the news. Asking a shallow question that someone says has never been seriously asked is another typical strategy of the Monkeys in media.

Capitalism was originally introduced as an alternative to Aristocratic and Plutocratic systems of Feudalism, where a family name determines one's future. A free economy is generally good. However, the single failure of Capitalism is that it gives more rights to corporations than to real humans, thus creating "corptocracy". For example, corporations are taxed after their expenses while humans are taxed before. And, corporations, which are simply pieces of paper, can pool the resources of many different people. After obtaining more money than any one person could every supply, and having more rights than humans, corporations that become large can economically "eat" and devour individual people as mythological giants eating common men.

Communism is the alternative that many take to Capitalism, without seeing the two-armed tactic.

Third options linger on the fringe, but never succeed, among them Austrian/Libertarian economics. No one considers that neither Capitalism nor Communism nor Libertarianism was ever engineered to succeed. No one considers Individualism as the preferable option.

Another "potted" control device is intellectual property rights. Copyrights and patents have a bias for corporations rather than individuals. While intellectual property and recognition for authors and inventors helps society, the main system of intellectual property enforcement hinders progress of science and useful art (while 'progress' was the legal basis for US intellectual property law). No one ever considers that, if a company does not use its patent, it should not be allowed to keep it. And, if a company buys a patent or copyright from the original inventor, that the original inventor should retain his own permission to use his invention without owing any royalties. Using and distributing other's intellectual property should be legislated in a manner that fits the natural human tendency to "use while giving credit", but neither of the two arms pursues this option either.

Other control devices include institutionalization of education, accreditation, and politics. Education is generally beneficial for society. But young children being away from their parents makes humanity weak. Once "organic farm certification" is regulated, it is easier for a company to bribe a politician into granting a certification that is not properly earned.

The Republican Party was created as a party that focused on individuals and, under the first Republican President, Lincoln, freed the slaves. Ironically, but not surprisingly when understanding the Monkey parable, the Republican party was commandeered after it was institutionalized and many Black Christians who believe in free market Capitalism tend to vote against Republicans, indicating that the Republican Party has long lost its identity. This is a clear example of the competitive two-armed approach of the Fallen Angels to keep people divided while claiming that "competition is somehow good". No one ever considers a non-centralized political party, such as *The People's Party*, a free eBook which explains a more in depth solution to two-armed politics. By having a single political party that allows politicians to have different values and beliefs, the people will be able to unite against the "Monkeys" and attain the 80% of commonly-shared public goals.

History is full of many other examples those who started to succeed, then were placed in a pot. Misery stories include new musicians, politicians, actors, businessmen, even teachers and religious leaders. As good causes begin to rise and gain recognition, they are approached by some group of people, fraternal organization, or secret society that poses to be good and share the same values. Thinking that they can't succeed without the help of others, these good and talented beginners agree to join forces with Monkeys who serve the Fallen Angels. This explains the self-destructive path of celebrities, the strange compromises of leaders in business and politics, and religious and educational establishments that keep their pupils constantly working, but never abundantly prosperous.

This parable explains Christian depression, divorce, and other compromise of their own beliefs after attending Sunday morning for many years. It also provides some explanation as to why people who don't attend Sunday morning gatherings can't stand many of those who enjoy the weekly meetings. The elevator doesn't go all the way to the top floor because the top floor can only be accessed by using the stairs—which is why the Monkeys say not to use the stairs. Christian leaders who compromise in even the smallest things will place their listeners in pots, making bonsai Christians who are never able to be happy because their growth seems to stop for no reason, while some trees always remain stronger.

The Monkeys in the jungle are the reason why it is absurd to choose one puppet over another, forgetting the puppet master. Choosing the Democrats as the alternative to the Republicans, or choosing the Republicans as the alternative to the Democrats, is as absurd as choosing one WWF pro celebrity over another. It is especially foolish to think that Libertarians were not designed by the Monkeys to attract dissidents, as the "third institution option", to keep "smart folk" under Monkey control.

It is equally absurd to choose the dropout, no-job, substance-addiction lifestyle as an alternative to seeking a master's degree—or vice versa. Both ends of the spectrum are part of the Monkey-controlled social hierarchy, which is the very purpose of the Monkeys in government trying to make every child attend an institutionalized school. While learning is good, placing consonants before and after one's name primarily serves the purpose of making everyone else feel inferior. If you have a master's degree, refuse to use the extra consonants and tell everyone that graduate school, even undergraduate, are paths necessary for a very small few.

Obsession with the top of the education system is a form of idol worship. This is the same reason that luxury brands place advertisements where they will be seen by people who will never buy their products: to "educate" people about how worthless they are, causing the 10% at the top to feel good about winning a false victory, and causing everyone else to obey those whom they have been conditioned to think are the "masters". Promoting this endless cycle of so-called "education" surmounts to nothing more than inferiority complex-based luxury marketing; the product is a low- six-figure income that still includes a mortgage.

Celebrating the upper echelon of institutionalized education is motivated by greed—a desire to earn money—and it only perpetuates the problem at the bottom of the scale because it was designed to be that way. None of this is by accident. Like a Ponzi scheme, big education was designed to fail 90% of its participants—rightly called "failing" because only a few actually become doctors, lawyers, professors, etc., while the rest "obey" the elites or else feel worthless—and often both. We were all better off as home-schooled farmers, learning and advancing society without being taken from our parents for this classroom show mislabeled as "education". Real education happens at home and from earthy rabbis like Jesus.

This is why Jesus commanded us not to use titles—because the real, un-institutionalized Jesus, the real

Teacher, knows about the Monkeys in the jungle and how we can escape them. If we don't use titles, then institutionalized hierarchies lose their power, top to bottom, and the tree finally escapes the pot of titles.

In religion, it is absolutely absurd to exit from traditional Fundamentalist Churchianity only to enter the Emergent Church movement (or whatever the latest hippie-like fad happens to be,) then to change again to secular Humanism—and deny the inherency of Scripture or that Jesus is the son of God—as if changing between any of these three is meaningful. All three are puppets with their strings being pulled by the Monkeys.

The Churchianity culture incorporates the Bible into its structure, but in a bland and powerless way, thereby serving the two-option purpose of either making people think less of the actual Bible (which is only partially and inaccurately represented and defended in Churchianity) or else to cause those who stay in Churchianity to remain weak, powerless, ignorant, controlling, and, frankly, annoying. This is intended to feed the economies of watered-down, non-Fundamentalist Western religion and secular humanism as a whole.

Consider the role the Bible has in this jungle... It has been exploited by the Monkeys, almost as bait. But the Bible itself was written by authors who were not controlled by the Monkeys. The Bible is God's light to guide our path to exit the jungle and thrive in the fields He created for us. Consider those who claim that the Bible was made up—those very critics are sold-out to the education institutions. The Bible is the one element in the jungle that is not controlled by the Monkeys. The only lie that the Monkeys made concerning the Bible is that the Bible itself was supposedly a lie.

The Bible is our last and best hope to sort out the jungle's confusion. Trying to discredit the Bible was yet another Monkey-made puppet, intended to make people think that there is no escape from the jungle at all—to cause utter despair. Fortunately, the credibility of the Bible has been well-documented and published. This evidence is available for those who are interested in finding it. There is no reason to run to Humanism as a supposed "alternative" to the Monkeys—they control that too. This is an example of a "loonie fringe 'third'".

All three corners of Western religious institutions remain part of institutionalism. They were engineered from their beginnings to seem interesting at first, but then to make people hungry and dissatisfied, with the goal to make people think that changing between these scripted institutions would be anything but futile. The same applies to religious institutions in and from other cultures. To escape captivity in the jungle requires us to know Jesus. And to know Jesus requires knowing Him unfettered, un-institutionalized, unbranded, and un-potted.

All the battles and options of the jungle are scripted, rehearsed, and organized by one mastermind group of Monkeys, to keep the people distracted from the very Monkeys who control them. The only escape is to escape contrived institutionalism itself—to leave the jungle. And only Jesus—the real Jesus—knows the narrow exit.

It is especially important for Christians to understand this Theorem and parable because Christians have the power to escape the Monkeys. The Fallen Angel, aliased "Lucifer", considers Jesus to be his primary enemy because the real, un-institutionalized Jesus earned the greatest power as the "suffering messiah" at the Cross. The same power is in the hands of Christians who know Jesus without institutionalized Churchianity.

The Monkeys are trapped in their own jungle and even they need help in order to escape. After all, the Monkeys didn't make the jungle, the Fallen Angel did. The Monkeys were merely his most convenient victims. Christians must not only escape from the Monkeys, they must help the Monkeys escape from themselves.

We don't need to hate the Monkeys. We don't need to try to kill them or punish them. God has already planned to burn the jungle. But first, all His children, including the Monkeys who want to escape, but don't know how, must get to safety. The sooner we evacuate the jungle—repentant Monkeys included—the sooner the jungle will burn. This is why vengeance must remain the Lord's work while spreading good news must remain ours.

There are many stories of people who climbed within those "Monkey" societies, only to find that their God is known as "Lucifer" when they reach the highest levels of ascension. But when they leave peacefully, in love, without slander, and by surrendering to Jesus, they are able to successfully exit without retribution. It is as if Jesus is the only alternative that the Monkey's have respect for, but this has comes with conditions of maintaining peace and not competing directly with the Monkeys in force or conflict.

Conclusion

This parable and Theorem explain how evil moves from one rising star to another, like a constantly shifting parasite. It explains how many of the scripted answers circulating in society have no hope of providing long-term solutions. Humans have the only power on the earth to create anything new. Monkeys and Tigers can only steal. When humans create something good, but then institutionalize it, the effort dies, leaving a large, empty shell. Then, the Monkeys inhabit that shell like a hermit crab who lives in an conch that he could not make on his own.

The system of control is the two-armed tactic with a third-option "curse" managed by the evil, spiritual fallen Watchers—the Fallen Angels who rebelled from the Lord. It also uses "potting" that allows trees to move, to be artificially appear taller by hoisting them, and creates an invisible ceiling merely by constraining roots. Their system claims to have the "secrets to success" and uses its stolen resources as supposed "evidence" to justify their advice.

The way to escape this control system is to avoid the lie that institutionalization is a "necessary evil" and to remain informal and organic in any and every way possible. While some institutions can't be avoided, effort should be made to exit from any institutionalized way of doing things.

Solutions include spending large amounts of time in prayer, to have Christian fellowship by informally talking about the Bible and Jesus with other Christians as a habit rather than on a weekly attendance schedule, and to promote laws that value human rights above rights of corporations, rather than only addressing human rights as matters for minorities. To do this, one must recognize the two-armed, third-option curse method and not become drunk on anger at one hand to the point where one serves the other hand in an attempt to "retaliate"; fur such is the goal of the approach.

Learn to recognize counterfeits for what they are. Don't despise the real Jesus merely because the devil wore a "Jesus" mask when he created his mischief. Be smarter than the Monkeys, but do not seek to kill them or imprison them. Metaphorically, the Monkeys were originally human, but morphed when they began to serve the Tigers. They can repent, but will probably only do so if normal people continue to do good things, thus starving the Monkeys of new trees to pot and steal.

One of the great questions termed "the problem of evil" asks why a good God allows bad things to happen. While this old question is addressed in many other works, the short answer is that God allows the worst things to happen to Himself because He is not indifferent to our pain, but patiently waits for each human to repent and walk away from serving evil. God does not annihilate evil because He is waiting for humans to reach the conclusion that evil is, under no circumstances, "necessary". The idea of "evil" being "necessary" is a contradiction between mutually exclusive concepts. As long as good men believe that "necessary evils" exist, God will allow evil to continue. The belief that "necessary evils" exist is, itself, a moral compromise. If people refused to compromise with evil, then there would be no way for the Fallen Angels to create mischief in the earth.

It has been said again and again, especially in recent history, that the mere daily deeds of ordinary folk are all that is necessary to stop the darkness. Evil prospers when good men focus on sports more than politics, when honest people compromise in the little things, when Christians either pray or work rather than both praying and working, when good men accept the term "necessary evil", and when people take vengeance, these things only feed evil when we should be forgiving and farming.

###

About the Author

Jesse Steele is an American writer in Asia who wears many hats. He learned piano as a kid, studied Bible in college, and currently does podcasting, web contenting, cloud control, and brand design. He likes golf, water, speed, music, kung fu, art, and stories.

Jesse owns various brands, occasionally teaches writing and piano, and preaches the evangels of Linux, Open-Source, and Jesus.

Poetry is code.™

Email: books@jessesteele.com
books.jessesteele.com

www.ingramcontent.com/pod-product-compliance
Lightning Source LLC
Chambersburg PA
CBHW030538220526
45463CB00007B/2891